P9-EKE-045

Hong Kong Poems by Gary Geddes

A number of these pieces have appeared in *Event* and *Border Crossings*, for which I thank the editors. I have also had the pleasure of seeing the entire narrative produced on stage at the University of Winnipeg, directed by Per Brask and performed and mounted by students from the Department of Theatre and Drama.

I am indebted to the whole library of memoirs, journals, novels, popular and military histories and journalism that has gathered around the Pacific war, particularly that relating to the fall of Hong Kong. Most important were the testimonies of the veterans themselves, given to me personally or made available to me on tape by the Aural History Section of the Museum of Man and Nature in Winnipeg or in written form through books such as Grant S. Garneau's *The Royal Rifles of Canada in Hong Kong*.

I would also like to thank the Canada Council for assistance in the early stages of this work and the University of Alberta for tolerating a brief absence in 1977 that first brought me to Hong Kong.

ISBN 0 88750 673 9 (hardcover)
ISBN 0 88750 674 7 (softcover)

Typesetting and design by Michael Macklem

Printed in Canada

PUBLISHED IN CANADA BY OBERON PRESS

This book is dedicated to my uncle, Tom Turner,
who fell from the sky into captivity,
but found his way home.

PREFACE

Some time early in 1975, when the Manitoba winter was at its worst, my friend Doug Elias left his job at the Museum of Man and Nature in Winnipeg to make his annual pilgrimage to the sea. As I was living in Victoria, about as far west and south as a Canadian can get without losing his identity, Elias paid me a call. I was glad to see him and I remember some pleasant talk around a quantity of good scotch. Lapsed Mennonites are an interesting lot and Elias was no exception. As I spoke briefly about my latest work and my interest in the dark zones of the Canadian conscience, Elias shifted his considerable weight on the couch and began to twist the ends of his huge black beard with both hands, like a man who wants to talk.

I don't recall his exact words on that night, but I remember the force with which he hooked me into his "story." Later, I was to see him as one in a long line of land-locked Ancient Mariners stationed at regular intervals along my life-line, whose messages would so profoundly determine what I wrote and how I conducted my life.

Elias told me of 1975 soldiers, one for every year of the Christian calendar, thrown away, pawns to the vanity of their leaders, the bungling of bureaucrats and the indifference of elected officials. Two battalions, untrained, ill-equipped, as hastily forgotten as they were despatched, fighting an impossible battle against crack Japanese troops, surviving defeat and the POW camps only to be faced with an equally intransigent adversary in the Canadian government and Department of Veterans Affairs.

One anecdote from Elias' dream-script that has stayed with me ever since concerns a young researcher from the Aural History Section at the Museum, who went out to interview a Hong Kong veteran on his farm. She found him in the fields on a Massey-Harris tractor, a huge man who looked like Moses or one of the prophets, a sort of bearded Gibraltar. When she introduced herself and explained the nature of the project, she was not prepared for the terrible silence that ensued or for the single tear that released itself from the left eye of this colossus and slid into the mat of black whiskers, leaving a clear track in the dust on his cheek.

I was not prepared for Elias' story either or the demands it would place upon me. He left shortly afterwards, mission accomplished, the albatross he had given me hanging from my back like a medicine bundle, or a rocket-launcher. I haven't seen him since, but I have thought of him often as I scrambled over rocks, beaches and tombstones in Hong Kong, as I poured over books and tapes in the libraries and archives, even as I went AWOL from my writing when the nightmares started.

I hope I have acquitted myself well of Elias and those two shades who met in the Manitoba wheatfields and that I have done justice to the courage and endurance of the men of the Winnipeg Grenadiers and the Royal Rifles of Canada. Their story required of me some hard lessons in archaeology, digging deeply as I did into history and then even more deeply into myself. What I have drawn from conversations, books, archives and the recesses of my own heart and imagination is part fact, part fiction, but true, I hope, to the spirit of events.

GARY GEDDES

Our reinforcements were mainly in the shape of very large Canadians, who looked quite able to go out and win the war with a set of brass knuckles. It was Christmas, however, and they were homesick for snow. "O Jesus, fellows! The kind that sits all over the trees like cotton." And food . . . (*Underground from Hong Kong* by Benjamin Proulx).

They were magnificent men, lacking nothing but the training suitable to their task of fighting in the Hong Kong hills. Unfortunately, a bureacratic error sent all their transport down to Australia (*The Hidden Years* by John Luff).

It must be said here and now that, through no fault of their own, these regiments added little to the lustre of Canada. They were despatched to Hong Kong at a week's notice after a long period of stagnation as garrison troops in the West Indies and Newfoundland respectively . . . . Their appearance on the island prompted a senior staff officer, among whose virtues tolerance was not the most prominent, to say they were "straight off the trees" (*The Fall of Hong Kong* by Tim Carew).

1

Rising sun

is a habit of mind
appearing over the edge
of the Atlantic each morning
to the weary garrison,
raw Township boys
and hoary vets of the last war
with no use for astrology

is nuclear fission, constant emission
of heat, light & radioactivity

is symbol painted on steel plates
just above the waterline of a passenger ship
in Manila Harbour, bull's eye
to Johnny Canuck
en route to Hong Kong

is eight minutes ahead of itself,
given the distance and speed
of light

is a flag in a shop window
in Wanchai, looking like a huge fried egg
to passing POWs,
the last egg they'll see
for $3\frac{1}{2}$ years

KRAVINCHUK

We're out back
of the reservoir
when this Nip plane
comes over the ridge
and opens fire.
As the shells hit
a trail of dust devils
snakes toward us
across the valley.
We stand gaping
like a couple of yokels
until it's just about
overhead, then dive
into the makeshift bunker.
Harris starts screaming
I'm hit, I'm hit,
O god, Sam, you can
feel the warm blood
on my shoulder.
His tragic look
is so authentic
you'd think
he'd rehearsed it
from old movies.
He'd have run off
screaming like that, too,
if I hadn't grabbed
both his ankles
and shouted:
Tea, you stupid fucker,
tea. I spilled the thermos
down your back.

9

GYSELMAN

Among the documents
you'll find a picture of me
standing on a railway tie
at the Winnipeg station,
a cigarette in my fingers.

The puff of smoke I exhale
looks like Scotch thistle
on my tunic lapel.
My face has the arrogant leer
of an evangelist.

Two months later
a quarter of us would be wounded
or dead and I'd dream nightly
of rats
eating dead Japanese.

2

The *Awatea* and *Prince Robert* have just set sail from Vancouver Harbour. Of course, the expression "set sail" is an anachronism in this age of steel turbines, but no-one is thinking about such fine discriminations of language as the ships swing into First Narrows and head toward the Lions Gate Bridge.

Irene has driven to the docks to watch the ships and now she is driving past Lost Lagoon in a small blue coupé with her father and two sons, one seven years old and reading a book in the back seat, the other sixteen months and standing in her lap twisting her nose and lips. Offers have been increasing since she won the contest as Miss Wrigley Spearmint Gum, but this is her day off work as a demonstator at Eaton's and she's determined to enjoy herself.

"Mummy, where are the ships going?"

"Nobody knows." Earnest face turned up from its book. Enough to break your heart.

"Well, how will the captain know which way to steer?"

The captain, a good question. Was he the officer who winked from the gangplank? Handsome men in their tight blue uniforms. The decks awash with soldiers, waving, whistling. The tune the band struck up was "Good Night, Irene." And the women? More than just grief in their faces. At least Ann and I have our men safely at home.

Topside, there's a soldier leaning against the gunmount of the quarterdeck. Pain has begun in his lower abdomen he will dismiss as seasickness. As it worsens, he'll seek medical help but be accused of malingering. Dying, he'll hear waves pound against the hull and the steady, rhythmic beat of the engines.

Several officers of C Force are in the mess discussing the missing transport vehicles and the mutton mutiny of the previous day, when soldiers tried to disembark to protest against the cramped quarters and greasy fare. A massive court martial is dismissed as too disruptive to morale. The YMCA officer sits apart, thinking of his wife and Homer's verses on the Trojan horse, while the ship carves its lethal way through the waters of Burrard Inlet.

The coupé has reached the end of the parkway now and moved onto the bridge, just as the bow of the *Awatea* comes abreast of the span.

"Did Daddy and Grandpa build those ships?"

She looks at her father, the other Grandpa, pipe in his teeth, conscious of the immense bulk passing below. Even above the smoke, she smells the grime on him, a smell that has engulfed her childhood, her entire life. Trips back and forth to small farms on Lulu Island, then to the docks. Buckerfield Seeds.

"Mother, will the ships sail away over the horizon?" The cowlick above his high forehead wobbles.

"Yes, dear, perhaps as far as China. Tonight, we'll look at the atlas and make up a story about it." Don't let anything escape you, Reenee, this is your day off: pipe smoke, salt air, grain, ripe diapers.

"Will they all die, Grandpa? Uncle too?"

"What's this nonsense?" Words divide around the clenched pipe-stem, re-form. "Of course they won't all die."

DALZELL

Tried selling in Toronto
but never made a dime.
Took off on freights
with eight other guys
for North Bay,
but the bulls kicked us out.
Had to work on a road gang
in Capriol for rations.
Got organized in '33
with a soup-kitchen on Water Street,
two meals a day.
Harvested a while,
worked as a cook at Shilo.
After the march to Ottawa
the camps were broken up.
Did sweat work for CPR
at Kenora in '35,
bought an Indian's tent
and camped out.
Married a widow with kids
in 1936 in Winnipeg.
Worked in woodyards,
cleaned streets for 20 cents
an hour plus meals.
Rent was $14 a month.
That's why I joined up.

Hell, we had none of that Depression crap.
Us boys were in a spending mood
and, by god, we'd transform the economy
overnight, changing dollars into wine,
feeding the four million Chinese
(or was it two then?).
No cheapskates in D Company,
not like the bloody Limeys.
Workers, blokes who never had twopence
back home in Leeds or Manchester,
hired Chinese coolies for a dime
to make beds, wash socks,
and rode through the streets
in rickshaws like the King.
It made you want to puke.
So you can understand
why we chose the Sun Sun Café,
which the Brits never patronized,
just a few Rajputs and Punjabis.
We were in high gear, knocking them back
and singing "Roll Me Over in the Clover,"
so no-one noticed the English NCOs
come in and start hustling the girls.
Suddenly this overweight Limey
insults the beaver. I could hear
muscles tighten in a hundred backs.
His mate tries to stifle him,
but someone at the next table
picks up the refrain
and goes on about colonials
being beaver-fuckers
and not knowing one end from the other,

which is why they're all under-endowed.
When the last Limey dragged himself outside,
we threw the Wurlitzer down the stairs
after him, still playing.
The proprietor never said a word.
He was standing on the bar
cheering us on. The guy
had relatives in Vancouver
with apartments on Commercial Drive,
so we were A-okay. By god,
if the Japs had attacked that night
instead of the next morning,
we'd have driven them back up the ass
of Colonel Tanaka. Nobody
insults the beaver.

15

WARNING TO LITERARY FIFTH COLUMNISTS

What I'm doing here is not writing,
but rewriting; and you're neither listening
nor reading, but quietly deconstructing this poem
I've worked so bloody hard on. Harold Bloom
calls it "aftering" or "creative misreading,"
fancy words for plain theft.
You're not the least bit interested
in how I think or feel or express myself;
what you want to know is how to eliminate me
and my words and replace them with your own version
of things, escape your fallen self
and take revenge on time. Well, watch out.
I didn't read *Poetry and Repression*
just for fun. Because I know your plans
and because I have no intention of being supplanted
by you or your rival text, I've mined this poem
with booby-hatches, trapdoors, pitfalls
and anti-reduction devices. Twenty crossbows
are set to fire when the main door opens.
This poem should give you such anxiety of influence
you'll want to gather and burn every copy
as a petty triumph over the inimitable.
That avenue's covered too;
you might as well go home and run a bath.
There'll be no iconoclasm today, no breaking

of the vessels. You can catalogue compulsively,
scribble psyches, and remake archetypes, even try
defensive irony as a means of aesthetic limitation;
but it won't work. This text is armed to the teeth
against all eventualities; free leave has been cancelled
and all eyes are fixed on the shifting horizon.
We'll fight until the tropes come home.
What, you ask, does Harold Bloom say
about subversion from within the poem itself?
Harold who?

3

Close-up of soldiers on duty
in 1941 at Shamshuipo Camp.
They pose on steps, one at ease,

one at attention, two kneeling,
and grin for the photographer
who might have been a friend.

Knapsacks over chests, rifles diagonal
from right hip to left shoulder.
One remembers the stranger

in the men's washroom at Regina,
who gave him fifty dollars, a uniform
and a new identity, then went AWOL

out of the train station, wearing
striped overalls and boots with no socks.
One anticipates a rendezvous later

at the Sun Sun Café in Wanchai:
red silk dress and almond skin.
One forgot to polish his boots

and hopes the duty officer won't notice.
One has nothing in his head
that might be called a thought,

yet he too smiles. Four Canadians
on duty. What you notice first
is the length of the bayonets.

HENDERSON

I did most of my fighting in Repulse Bay
in a hotel half-full of civilians.
We took up positions in a plush suite
on the second floor.

One of the men sat in an armchair
scanning hills out back with binoculars.
When he spotted movement, I'd swing
into the window and fire, then drop back.

Suddenly there was a woman in the doorway,
saying, My dog, I'm looking for water for my dog.
We pulled her down out of the line of fire
and gave the dog radiator water we used for tea.

Later, when the Japanese were two football fields away
and their planes were dive-bombing the barracks,
I thought of that woman and her parting comment:
If he bothers you by barking, shoot him.

19

SULLIVAN

There's a strange hush at St. Stephen's
as we wait for them to storm the College.
Nurses drift like butterflies among the injured,
offering a word, a touch, a cigarette.
When the enemy bursts through the door

I'm lying on a cot at the far end of the corridor,
my head bandaged, my leg supported in a sling.
Two soldiers proceed to bayonet the sick and wounded
in their beds, to a chorus of screams and protests.
A nurse throws herself on top of one of our boys

to protect him—it might have been the kid
from Queen's—and they are both killed
by a single thrust of the bayonet.
I suppose they were sweethearts. Pinned
at last, she does not struggle. Her hands

open and close once, like tiny wings,
and the dark stain on her white, starched uniform
spreads like a chrysanthemum, a blood-red sun.
I cut the cord supporting my leg, slip on
the nearest smock and stand foolishly at attention,

making the salute. My right index finger
brushes the damp cotton of the bandage.
Later, the butchers are shot by their own officers;
one, apparently, had lost a brother
in the final assault.

20

CURRY

I recall a rice paddy back of Kowloon,
a temple set in the middle.
Mountains in the background are faded,
but more advanced rice stands out
in rows above the water.

Overturned wicker baskets
are used as tables to display produce.
When they don't contain bok choi
or onions, they display the small
round face of a child.

21

4

I spent several mornings in the office of the *South China Morning Post*, reading copies of *Hong Kong News*, produced after the Japanese victory on Christmas Day in 1941. Early sun glinted off the high-rises and office towers in Victoria as I crossed on the Star Ferry and a huge Bayer Aspirin sign on the roof of a building confirmed my impression of the Crown Colony as a colossal headache.

I was staying in an unheated room in Chungking Mansions on Nathan Road, Kowloon-side, a high-rise slum that offered a rich assortment of internationals selling silk, sex and semi-precious gems. Ascending in the creaking elevator, you witnessed a discontinuous film-strip of erotic tableaux, heated arguments and half-finished transactions.

The cluster of rooms on the seventh floor was bucolic by contrast and had an air of exhausted camaraderie that surprised me, a tribute to the two families of Chinese who ran the place. My room looked out on an alley, a dark, awesome abyss that separated me from the balconies and opulent suites of the Holiday Inn. For only four dollars a night, I could switch my lights off and, unobserved from my window, watch the comings and goings in those expensive rooms. Or I could gaze at the stars through a cloud-cover of laundry hanging out to dry on the floor above.

I soon tired of both astrology and low-grade voyeurism and made the rounds of the local bars, particularly the Ship's Inn, run by a Vietnam veteran who'd parlayed his injuries and discharge into a small fortune on the black market. He'd also developed certain tastes that only the Orient could satisfy.

Jim was curious about my mission in Hong Kong, gathering information about Canadians killed or incarcerated there during the war. He ventured it was only non-combatants who wrote about the war. I nursed my glass of bitters and thought of Wilfred Owen, Charles Yale Harrison, even the Royal Rifles' own William Allister. Jim's stitch-marks ran from one ear down across his throat to the other shoulder, like a tiny rope ladder on a helicopter. I said I supposed he was probably right.

5. SONG OF THE BARBED WIRE

I make my first appearance in this legend
east of Wainwright, along the Fifth Concession,
stretched between poplar poles, staples
pounded in to keep me taut.

I was taught all right, taught to do a job—
containment—so I practised on buffaloes,
then on German POWs, lucky if they'd known,
cooped and insolent in tropical gear
near Kingston Town.

I graduated with Honours, trotted out
my scrolls for public scrutiny.

Untroubled by loyalty or scruples,
I served both sides at once: those boys
who jeered their inmates in the tropics
now are jailed themselves, their shaggy mains
not worth a Yankee nickel in this caper.

A little culture rubs off on me, a little flesh,
sins of commission, small retainer fees.
I turn up at the trials in Tokyo drunk,
unstrung, offering to keep the sun in check.

I know my first concession
will be my last.

JOKE FOR THE DAY

INTERNMENT is a great social leveller.
Peakites and Kowloonites are now rubbing shoulders.

PROULX

I was a stockbroker and amateur jockey,
so I spent a lot of time at Happy Valley
and the Club. Ottawa was a long way off.
I knew the market price of commodities
like trust. Hong Kong was down the drain.
So that's how we went too, right out

the storm sewers to a waiting vessel.
Marsman and I escaped and both wrote books
about it. Others were not so lucky.

Three men captured were imprisoned 21 days,
made to dig their own graves, then shot.
Payne, Berzenski, Adams and Ellis

were caught boarding a sampan, interrogated
by Inouye, beaten and promptly shot.
Three hundred Hong Kong dollars

could not keep us afloat on that market
and we had to swim
the last three miles to China.

ANDERSON

One of the jobs I had
after emigrating from Sweden
was in the freezer department
at Swift's, shipping
cheap meat and bacon to Japan.

Military life was good.
When the Pats discharged me
as an alien, I signed up
with the Grenadiers and said
I was born in Alberta.

There's hardly a thing
the Chinese didn't invent.
You name it: noodles, paper,
printing, the compass,
even gunpowder, yet
they had to step off sidewalks
to let the British pass,
then the Japanese.

Major Boone shaved his head
and bowed to the rising sun.

26

HARDY

I belonged to the millionaires' club.
You know, guys like Ross and Clarke
from Montreal. One of them owned
Great Lakes Steamships; the other
flew his own cook to Hong Kong
and put him up in a Kowloon hotel.

Me, I was eating a cheese sandwich
on my lunch hour from Eaton's
when I saw the recruiting banners.
This sergeant buttonholes me and says:
Join the Grenadiers and winter in Jamaica.
What the hell, I thought, why not?

I cycled over to Main Street,
was driven to the Minto Armouries
and given a uniform.
Mother couldn't believe it;
neither could I.

Such a big-time spender, I left my bike
against a lamppost in the street.
I went back to Eaton's after the war.
Why did it happen? Don't ask me,
that's not my department.

6

The prime minister knew what Churchill said
concerning the defence of Hong Kong.
He wrote the words more or less verbatim
in his diary:

> Let us devote ourselves to what is possible.
> Japan will take Hong Kong, beyond the shadow
> of a doubt, when the time comes. Think
> only of a presence.

Symbolic garrison, that was
the operative phrase.

But he knew, also, the words
of a mother in Moose Jaw
who would not release the hand
he extended until he heard
her thoughts about the war:
a farm dying from neglect,
while husband and son
rotted in the Yorkshire rain.

He did not bother to tell her
they were among the ranks
that booed his presence
in their midst in England.

He saw blood. Privately,
of course. And it was blood
he knew would bring them round
to the war effort.
The blood of mothers' sons
spilled on foreign soil.

So he gave the nod to Crerar
and prayed forgiveness
from his dearest Mum.

29

DISTINGUISHED SERVICE DECORATIONS

Pellagra
is a vitamin-deficiency disease
that produces sores on the skin,
red and weeping sores, as well as ulcers
on the lips, gums, tongue and throat.

It also has a tendency to cause
severe irritation and chafing
around the genitals. Thus
the nickname: Rice Balls
and Strawberry Balls.

The three Ds of pellagra are
dermititus, diarrhoea, dementia.

BOWEN ROAD HOSPITAL

I've seen temporary loss of memory in lads
after a raid. Simple inhibitory response
of the brain to excessive stress.
Sleep reduces intellectual activity,
letting the brain and nervous system rest.
Withold sleep for an extended period,
or interrupt it, and you break down
these inhibitory factors. Drugs
might have worked well enough
if we'd had any to administer.
He seems to have lost consciousness
after the Japanese bayoneted him
and pushed him down an embankment.
Who's to say he was lucky?
He turned at the last moment
and deflected the blow as it grazed
one rib and then made a real mess
of the muscles and bone in the upper arm.
We had to take it off just below
the shoulder. He awakened at night
to the sound of shells exploding everywhere.
He was already weak from loss of blood
and could barely extricate himself
from under the weight of a dead comrade,
let alone crawl toward safety, wherever
that might be. When they brought him in
he was in shock. Bomb happy, they call it.
Aural stimuli, such as grenades and bombs,
had caused reflex inhibitions in other areas,
so he had this fixation on getting out

and rejoining his company, at any cost,
with no thought for the deplorable state
he was in. When we ran out of gin,
he had to be restrained. Unfortunately,
this fixed state of excitation gave way
to a pathological level of inertia
that would have been more or less permanent,
if blood-poisoning hadn't taken him first.

32

BERTULLI

It was a carry-over
from the class system back home.

The officers never overcame
their elitist training;
not even imprisonment
could make us equal.

Take the MO, for instance.

An excellent doctor in the field,
but after the war, as far as I
could figure, he sold us out
for a cushy government job.
He was a chocolate soldier,
a fraternity boy who took courses
to qualify as major.

Nobody knew our medical histories
better than he did: blindness,
heart failure, mental breakdown,
suicide. But where was his voice
in the debate for compensation,

hundred percent pensions?

VARLEY

We were an odd lot, with Orville Kay,
a crown attorney, as CO
and under him petty criminals
he had sent to Stony Mountain,
crime-sheets long as your arm.

They lacked nothing in courage
and were as devoted to Crawford
as anyone in sick-bay, myself
included. The Commandant
used to lecture us and blamed
all deaths on the orderlies
and medical personnel.
One day he beat Crawford badly
about the head and shoulders
and threatened to behead anyone
who claimed to be doing his best.

I don't know what came over me,
but I found myself stepping forward,
shaking Crawford's hand, and
following the sergeant out back.

The Commandant was impressed
and things eased off after that,

for a time.

CRAWFORD

I started with a billiard table
for operations. No supplies,
no drugs. Everywhere you looked
men were making apparatus.
Wilcox found a damaged straight razor
and spent two days removing the gouge
with a stone. It was all ad hoc.
An eye-chart to do visual acuities,
with Chinese ink on white paper;
and a dingus to measure peripheral vision.
Then they made an adjustable table
and an ingenious peanut-oil lamp:
reflectors concentrated the light.
The Japanese idea of health care
was to send us gallons of Lysol:
keep camp clean, no disease.
Quarantine for dysentery was one strand
of barbed wire; diphtheria, two.
Selwyn Clark managed to smuggle in
some thiamin in a Prayer Book
with help from interpreter Watanabi,
so we had a little Vitamin B
for the worst cases of beriberi.
Some men kept their feet on tiles
or out of windows to cool them.
Others used to soak their feet
for relief; however, this softened
or mascerated the skin, so infection
could set in, then gangrene.
It meant patrolling
the latrines.

7

—Sir, I can't go.
—I know, Jim, you're too sick. I'll send Al.
—You can't do that, Sir. He's worse off than I am.
—I have to send someone.
—I'll go.

36

MALLORY

Work party again at 6 AM. Low-lying fog over the harbour as we board the ferry that takes us from Shamshuipo to Kai Tak. Bitter cold. Can see only the Peak over Victoria now. No wonder money builds high up, a hedge against fire, flood, disease, the poor.

I'm working alongside Deslile, who can barely raise his shovel, never mind singing in his perfect tenor voice. The poor devil has been down in sick-bay for weeks with dysentery and electric feet. The grey skin is stretched over his bones like kite paper. I try to cover for him by working a little faster than usual, but I know I can't keep up the pace. There must be a hundred of us working on the Reclamation, dumping earth from the high ground to extend the runway into the sea. You have to keep moving or freeze.

"Dumby, speedo!" The guards are shouting to our left, trying to make better time. I suppose they get more rations if the work goes well and a few extra inches are gained each day.

I fill Deslile's baskets as lightly as I can and help him up with them. He moves off ahead of me, so thin he looks as if he might crumble under the weight. The concentration required to put one foot ahead of the other must be enormous, but he plods toward the fabricated shoreline. He's not quite over the dysentery and the backs of his legs are stained from the thin bile that passes through him. He resembles a mechanical scale, the two baskets suspended from the ends of a pole at slightly different levels at his sides.

If we can make it to the edge without attracting attention, no-one will notice the size of his load. We are only twenty yards from the water when one basket dips below knee-level and brushes the ground. It's just enough to betray him. He falls straight forward on his face. The wicker baskets, unfortunately, remain upright and reproachful beside him.

I stand at attention, my legs aching under the weight. Deslile does not move. I think his heart has given out, but I can hear him whisper.

"Je m'excuse, Alvin. Je m'excuse."

Two guards are kicking and shouting. They drag him to his feet and knock him back and forth between them like a rag doll. One of them reaches into a half-filled basket and throws a handful of dirt into his face. The closed eyes seem to infuriate him as much as the baskets.

"Dumby, cheat. No good."

Deslile's bowels choose that moment to discharge, though he has eaten nothing for days. It's a miracle of creation, or of criticism: *e nihilo fecit*. The guard's face contorts and he strikes Deslile in the mouth with his rifle butt. Then they are dragging him to the water's edge. All work on the Reclamation has stopped. He is on his knees and has begun to sing one of those folksongs that have followed us from Sherbrooke to Newfoundland across Canada and aboard the *Awatea*. I can feel my legs giving out and the bamboo pole cutting into my shoulders. The fog is breaking up and sunlight reflects off the sword as it falls, repeatedly, on his neck. He's remained somehow on his knees and has to be pushed over. One of them kicks his head down the small embankment into the sea.

Several of us are detailed to dig a shallow grave and he is buried, headless, beneath the runway of the Kai Tak airport.

8

The Department of National Defence regrets that it cannot release medical documents, on the grounds that their contents might prove an embarrassment to the men and their families.

HONG KONG NEWS

There are male and female dragons
and they are different.

The male has rough, jagged horns,
deep eyes, wide nostrils, a pointed mane
and thickly growing scales.

The female has wavy-surfaced horns,
a flat nose, a smooth mane,
round eyes and thin scales.

While the strength of the male dragon
is in the upper part of the body,
the tail is the strongest part
of the female dragon.

9

By the end of the first week, I'd made the rounds
of all the well known battle sites,
including Gin Drinker's Line, Wong Nei Chong Gap,
Repulse Bay Hotel, St. Stephen's College
and half a dozen other spots mentioned in diaries
and official records. I took the funicular
to the Peak and made my way along the boardwalk
to the Mount Davis side, where I could look out
over Aberdeen, the reservoir, the floating city
of junks and the vast expanse
of the South China Sea. The hillside was covered
in spiky grass, small bushes and delicate wildflowers
of the orchid variety. I stumbled on a cave
large enough to hold a man. The hole in the ground
seemed a perfect correlative to the depression
I was in, so I spent several hours there
thinking about the meaning of loyalty in times
of war and peace and trying to imagine the feelings
of soldiers, beleaguered and outnumbered here,
so far from home and the familiar.
All I got for my troubles was a chill.
On the way down, I found a heavy chunk of metal
about twelve by twenty-four inches, with rust
forming around three shell-holes. Some blue paint
still clung to the slab. Foolishly, I left it

to the weather. I brought home, instead, articles
from the *Hong Kong News*, ironic pieces
making light of the Japanese victory and propaganda
designed to win over the Chinese to the idea
of A Greater Asian Co-Prosperity Sphere.
No easy task for the butchers of Nanking.
My co-tenants at the Chungking Mansions turned out
to be call-girls, working for an escort service
in Kowloon that catered to visiting businessmen.
Margaret, the English one, told me she preferred
Japanese men. Her other clients were wracked with guilt
and constantly argued about the price; not so,
the Japanese. They had class, treated the girls
to dinner, wine, sometimes an evening out.
Tradition, she explained to me. Yes, I knew something
about Japanese tradition, especially Bushido.
I maintained a casual, worldly air, but was really
quite shocked by such goings-on. Jim laughed
when I brought the subject up and made some joke
about hotel rooms for the poor with wall-to-wall pussy.
In Saigon, we called it keeping the world free
for democracy, he said, while his Adam's Apple
moved under the laddered scar like a grenade.
That night I drank too much and puked in the alley
between Chungking Mansions and the Holiday Inn.
And I dreamed of Margaret and the others
and their semi-precious gems.

41

DONNELLY

The real heroes of Hong Kong
were the cooks and comedians.

When we returned
half of us were impotent.
One vet committed suicide
two weeks after his marriage.
Porteous took 3000 milligrams
of niacine daily till he died.

All we ever talked about was food.
—Howard, did I ever tell you
about my mother's pecan pies?
—No, Jack, I don't think you ever did.
Of course it was the hundredth time.
After the war, Jack sent me
a bushel of pecans from Texas.

We kept recipe books
instead of girlie magazines.
We'd have traded *Playboy*
for *Betty Crocker*
any day.

MERRITT

Bastards stripped me of rank
for complaining of officers stealing food.
When I threatened to take it
to Brigadier Price of the Rifles
I got my stripes back quick.

What did we eat? We ate rats,
though they weren't plentiful,
a dachshund, runaway pigs
from a Jap lorry, garbage,
a Labrador retriever. Maybe

you'd scrounge crabs along the shore
at the steel works. Sometimes
we'd steal rice from the Japs
and cook it a little at a time
in the soup pot, wrapped in a sock.

I'd have eaten one of them, too,
given half a chance.

43

FERGUSON

I used to dream
of pork chops

and I saw Major McCauley's arm
blown off.

I went down
from 170 to 90 pounds;
no-one from back home,
not even the family,
recognized me.

O ya, and it cost 20 cents
to reach the barracks by rickshaw
after a Wallace Berry film.

Hell, I remember more
about the Halifax explosion.

LA FORTUNE

Rien à manger,
rien à dire.

44

10

"What's this?" The prime minister scans
a 32-page letter attacking the *Duff Report*.
"Drew must be crazy. Or underemployed.
Obviously, it's a cover-up;
you can't win elections,
or wars, for that matter,
with egg on your face.
He could spare me disclaimers
about not wanting scapegoats;
of course he wants them,
he wants the government
to fall into his lap.
Those poor devils who never tossed
a live grenade in training.
I'd have delivered them personally,
if they'd put one under you, George.
Spare me your lectures
on the nature and complexity
of the three-inch mortar;
and don't go on about Ralston,
water-carriers, McNaughton,
theatres of war. Homework, yes,
I'll give you credit for that.
But you're a bit sophomoric
in your displays of information.
Information ain't facts.
What do you know about 'evil influences'

at work in our midst, George?
I agree, Lyman Duff lacks subtlety.
He's too easily satisfied.
'Without a fighting chance'
—Hong Kong in a nutshell.
I envy you that one, George.
There's a bit of the old poet
in you, if a conservative one.
Your hockey analogy was not bad,
either:

> It would be just as reasonable to suggest
> that men could be called trained hockey
> players who had been shown a hockey-stick,
> a puck and goal-post and had their use
> explained to them, as it would be to say
> that men who had received lectures on weapons
> had actually been trained in the use of those
> weapons.

Not just Canadian content, George,
but a New Testament ring, to boot.
We could have used a man like you
on our side."

46

11

I don't suppose this information will be useful to you in your research, but I still have in my possession a letter written by my son, Private Andy Appleton, about three days after his arrival in Hong Kong. Apparently, he was on exercises in the New Territories—that's the section the Chinese want back in 1997—when he noticed the soil there was the same rust-red as here in Charlottetown, from all the iron deposits. He says he's putting a few grains in the envelope, but I guess the censors dumped it out when they cut out the names of several small villages. Maybe they thought someone would do a soil analysis and give away our positions. Anyway, Andy described various exotic flowers and plants in detail, including some sort of philodendron with huge, broad leaves the shape of tractor seats, the metal kind with sections cut out for ventilation or, perhaps, just to save steel. The picture he drew of the plant looked more like a skull, or one of those death's-head masks you see nowadays on goalies in the NHL.

Andy wouldn't have ended up dead in Hong Kong if I hadn't encouraged him to spend a summer in the Eastern Townships as an apprentice-surveyor for Lands & Forests. He met Paulette the same day he enlisted. She was working in one of those mobile chip-waggons near the armouries. Her father didn't approve of the war—he was some sort of nationalist—but he paid for the wedding and secretly wished Andy luck on his travels, toasting a victory from a small mickey of rye he kept on the rafters in the woodshed.

Andy may have been the first Canadian killed in action during World War II, but all he ever wanted to do was study plants. He was the kind of person who noticed things, correspondences. I'd like to think he got that from me. Paulette used to write to me during the war, but afterwards we lost touch. I knew what she looked like, though, from a snapshot

BERRIGAN

I'd been a teacher outside Yorkton,
so they put me in charge of the library.
There wasn't much variety,
so some guys had read the same books
a dozen times. After a while,
they began to notice the words.

Four titles come to mind
as having more than literary significance
for our situation. One was Maugham's
Of Human Bondage, a sort of case-book
for the physically and mentally lame POW.
Then there was *Down the Garden Path*.
Someone had crossed out the author's name
and written in Mackenzie King.

Cheating Death was certainly popular,
but nothing had so much appeal
as Seton's *Wild Animals I Have Known*.
The text was surrounded with marginalia,
every blank space crammed with expletives
and commentary, like biblical exegesis.
Seton was a Canadian and his stories
seemed to transport our captive audience
back home, even the stories set
in Nebraska and New Mexico.
I knew *Billy the Dog that Made Good*
and *Cute Coyote and Other Stories*
from my courses at teachers' college
in Saskatoon, but the all-time favourite

was "Lobo, King of Currumpaw," which describes
the capture and death of a wolf
after the killing of his mate, Blanca.
In the margin was scribbled: "Bullshit,
animals can't die of a broken heart."
Beneath that, in a very precise script:
"Don't be too sure, mate. Signed,
a fellow-animal."

I often wondered about Seton's association
with the Boy Scouts of America.
He accused them of being militaristic,
so they threw him out in 1915,
ostensibly for not being an American.

50

PORTEOUS

I consoled myself
with thoughts of my wife
and lines of poetry
I'd memorized at school.

The silence of Ajax
is more eloquent
than words.

That helped pass the night
in a drainage ditch,
watching tracers and fumes
from the hit refinery.
Then the waiting
and privations
made almost bearable
by concerts
I helped organize
in my official capacity
as YMCA officer.

Our fortunes lie
on the razor's edge,
O men of Iona;
submit to hardships,
you will have toil
for the moment,
but you will overcome
your fear.

51

Those are the words
of Dionysus in Heroditus.
While thoughts of her
kept me alive, my wife
had passed silently
into the dark.

250-WORD ESSAY REQUIRED BY THE JAPANESE ON THE BATTLE OF HONG KONG

On the southeastern shore of Lake Winnipeg, there's a small town called Libau. There wasn't much happening in those days to keep a town going, so we had to settle for a store, a garage and a barber-shop. The Japanese who took over the store in 1935 tried to sell sandwiches and coffee on the side and take in laundry, but nobody had money to pay for groceries, never mind the luxuries. After school, when my chores were done, I sometimes did odd jobs for Mr. Saeto in exchange for food. I piled wood, stocked shelves, or maybe brought him a catch of goldeye from the lake. The first time, I gutted them and cut off the heads and tails, but Saeto shook his head and made clear he wanted his fish intact. Kids used to say the Japanese ate fish-eyes as a delicacy, but I think Saeto used the head and tail for soup. He told me he had a wife in Japan and that he had been to visit her twice, the first time producing a son, the second time a daughter. I had a lot of respect for him when I heard that. Once, while we were warming our hands in front of the wood-heater, I asked him why he didn't bring his family to Canada. He told me politics was no good; it made people's hearts like stone. In all that time, I never even heard of Hong Kong.

249 words

BORZOV

Optic neuritis or retro-bulbar atrophy:
blindness by any other name.
It set in after the first draft of Canadians
to Japan.

       They were trying to raise
a freighter just off shore; the stern
emerged, but sank twenty minutes later.

I'd started sketching from my perch
near the barbed wire, but found
I could no longer gauge depth
or draw a straight line.

          The gaunt faces
of my friends seemed more distorted
than usual in the cold December air.

Several of those on work drafts were lined up
for inspection, wearing sun-glasses
they'd made out of wire and broken bottles.
The cock-eyed lenses and skinny bodies
gave them the look of pumpkins on sticks.
I remember them fading as if a curtain
had been pulled over my eyes.
I just sat there in the sunlight,

brushes in my hand, thinking about Mallory
and what he'd said to me after tenko.
You could hear the eerie notes of a Chinese flute
over the water.

Listen, he said, can't you hear it?
What? I said. Him, Deslile, still singing.
It's all that keeps me going, the knowledge
he won't stop singing.

54

12

From the offices of the *South China Morning Post*, I could
watch the shipping in the harbour. Freighters of every size
and registry lay at anchor, waiting to unload raw materials
and pick up manufactured goods, much of it produced aboard
the flotilla of junks that scooted like water-beetles over the
skin of the bay. On the nearest of these junks, I could make
out children going about their tasks. They were unschooled
but sea-wise, tending animals, small shipboard gardens, running errands and, when they were not baby-sitting, helping
at the sewing-machines and assembling gadgets or toys for
foreign kids who hadn't dirtied their hands with anything but
play. Floating factories that never stopped, despite the rota-
tion of the earth and the invention of the calendar.

Still, there was a freedom of sorts. These descendants of
traders and pirates, scorned and criticized for their unsavoury
aspect and links with crime, were the secret envy of many
underpaid and unprotected workers, who slept in shifts in the
overcrowded slum-rises. They had helped Proulx escape and
now many of them were running illegals from Vietnam, Cam-
bodia and Mainland. For all I knew, the junk I could see re-
fusing to give way to the Star Ferry and sending it off course
might be harbouring some precious human cargo, stowed
away amongst barrels of fuel oil and bales of cotton.

I'd have to tie things up soon. I had responsibilities to as-
sume back home in Edmonton. I'd left a note on my office
door that said, simply: GONE FISHING, IN HONG KONG. A lot
of weight hung on that comma. And there was the matter of
some articles I'd threatened to write for a friend at the *Journal*:
Britain's expiring lease on Hong Kong; the current state of
refugee camps; the night life and the black market.

"Why go to Hong Kong? You can get all the information
you need from the computer data-bank and imagine the rest."

We were sitting in the revolving restaurant of the Château Lacombe, across from his offices, while Edmonton disappeared under its annual snowfall. Two cars could not make the grade and were wedged, crosswise, on the road below. Everything was grinding to a halt. Me, too.

"I've got to get out of here. You're probably right about the book, but there are things I have to find out. Facts, you know, impressions. I've been writing journalism for so long, I've forgotten how to invent."

The waitress brought the refills we'd ordered and a bill. My friend was a regular, but never had more than two drinks, which he referred to as his lube-job. In a high-powered business that produced as much stress as information, he was a bastion of health and good sense. He'd been a good eighth man, a key, on the rugby team too. He was turning the drink in his hands and watching the amber liquid and ice gather momentum. When he stopped the glass, its contents continued their circuit of the container.

The junk had passed out of sight now, behind a high-rise under construction, one of those 35-storey human beehives that were replacing the 15-storey variety. Construction workers moved soundlessly on bare feet along the narrow planks and bamboo scaffolding, secured only with hemp.

BARDAL

You must be kidding,
we were heading the wrong way
up Corrigon Street.

Ya, ya, John Norris was beaten
by the Kamloops Kid.

You sure that thing's working?

I was an undertaker in Winnipeg
even before I joined up,
with all the jokes and cheap shots
the trade elicits. They stopped,
though, when the dying began.

Nobody wanted the photographs
and Hong Kong memorabilia
I'd collected over the years
and stored in a back room
with shoe-boxes full of unclaimed ashes.

You've gotta push both buttons,
the PLAY and the RECORD.

Prison camp had its good points,
at least you knew what to expect.
When liberation came,
they had to pry me loose.
Back home, I felt stifled and resentful
and fled to New York
to lose myself in crowds.

I carried dysentery for six months
and memories I couldn't bury.

58

INOUYE

They used to call me the Kamloops Kid
and talk behind my back in camp.
I was born beside an orchard
in the Interior and went to school
in the Valley, beautifully cultivated
in terms of land, but not people.
I couldn't wait to leave and pursue
a civilized education in Japan.
They assumed I was just getting even
for the abuse I took as a kid
in BC, dodging stones and insults
in the streets, being laughed at
and called a little yellow bastard
by the white gangs at harvest time.
After dark, I used to lob culls
into their midst around the campfire
like grenades and run like hell.
Actually, I got the shit kicked out of me
more often in the Japanese army
than at the hands of racists in Canada.
What finally broke my restraint was news
of the Evacuation, my mother and sister
in boxcars, like cattle, shunted

59

back and forth from Vancouver
to internment camps in the Interior.
I couldn't forgive those oversized bastards
for proving I was right, after all.
When I claimed immunity at the trials
in Tokyo, as a British subject,
the judge obliged by hanging me
in Hong Kong. Everyone
thought it a great
joke. Bad apple,
he said.

60

BATTEN

What's race got to do with it?
I was born in Liverpool
but came to Canada when I was two.

I started out on the Vickers,
500 rounds per minute.
Damn good gun, but a bit heavy.
Takes three men, one on the gun,
one on the tripod, all three
carrying boxes of ammunition.

I remember instructing a platoon
of Poles not long after I joined up
in '34—I was with the Pats.
By the time I finished with those guys,
they could assemble by touch in the dark.

Then we switched to the lighter Brens,
with 50 rounds per minute in the clip.

I made it through the fighting,
the camps, even the coal mines in Oyama;
then, coming home, the plane
hit an air-pocket over Honolulu
while I was in the can
and I broke my collar-bone
and three ribs.

13

Margaret asked me over breakfast if I'd store a suitcase for her in my room. She and her room-mate were in trouble with the Tongs for freelancing with clients and witholding money from the escort agency. They both expected a raid on the hotel, by the police or the underworld—it didn't matter which. I made some excuse about the possibility of a last-minute flight to Tokyo and not wanting to take responsibility for the stuff. Margaret smiled and said nothing further on the subject. I checked into the YMCA and made plans for a side trip to Lantau Island, two hours by boat from Hong Kong.

I wanted a sense of how things might have looked almost 40 years ago, when C-Force disembarked. It was raining on Lantau and the dirt roads were impassable, so I sat in a hovel eating soup and rice gruel and watching a Chinese martial-arts classic on black and white. I might as well have stayed at the Y.

Back at the dock, the rain had let up. I looked around at the assembled passengers. Several tiny grandmothers, bearing huge bundles, were tending one or more small children; a couple of teenagers in blue terylene slacks were tearing at strips of fat-fried bread, stoking up for a night in the sweatshops of Kowloon. Rubbish from Hong Kong Island nudged the pilings.

I was preoccupied with thoughts of the dangers Margaret was in and busy indulging in a little guilt for being such a shit, so I did not notice the apparition in batman cape and mediaeval scholar's hat, the floppy velvet kind with a narrow brim running the entire circumference, who must have preceded me aboard. As the terminal slipped astern, this bearded emanation confronted me, a thin, white arm emerging from beneath the cape to present a business card and receive mine. I mumbled an apology and introduced myself.

KARL A. B. HELMSTRAND scanned me with cold, blue eyes and a hawkish intensity. His card was replete with graphics and Chinese calligraphy, spelled out for the uninitiated: KARMA, DEJA, TASHI. And there was an address on Lantau Island. After a few perfunctory questions designed to size me up, the obligatory lecture began. If I wanted to know about Hong Kong and the war, I should learn about the Overstately Powers (here, a thick, white eyebrow rose one inch), particularly the Jews, who had started the war and were behind every international incident.

Much as I tried to concentrate on Helmstrand's lecture, I couldn't help thinking about Margaret and the trip we'd taken the previous day to one of the refugee camps on Kowloonside, not far from Kai Tak Airport. Inside the high metal fence and barbed wire, we were met by officials, quickly briefed and given over to the care of two refugee kids, a girl about eleven who took Margaret off for a tour of the dormitories and a one-armed boy in a Hawaiian shirt, the kind manufactured with the wrong floral designs in Korea. He could tell I was neither an adoptive parent nor someone from an agency, so he asked if I had any cigarettes or dope. I gave him the pack of Players I'd taken to carrying in Hong Kong as ice-breakers.

My unofficial ambassador was Vietnamese. His sister had been a prostitute and made a lot of money from the Americans, which she'd salted away for the end of the war. She planned to take Benno with her to California. Ten hours after the last helicopter dusted the roofs of Saigon, she was killed by the liberating troops, three of them raping her first and taking her wristwatch. Benno was denounced by school chums who wanted to ingratiate themselves with the victors; then, when he was spared, they tormented him and tried to force him to reveal the whereabouts of the money. He was cut up with a machete and left for dead. What saved him was a cotton headband he'd been given by a drunk Marine his sister had brought home one night. He wrapped that around the bleeding stump and twisted it tight with a screwdriver before passing out. When he woke, he was on the boat, wedged between two old people he'd never seen before, his new "family." The screwdriver and blue headband were gone, replaced by a stained bandage covering the stump, which had been charred to prevent infection.

Margaret was crying when I met up with her at the gate. "I'd like to take them all home," she said, dabbing at her eyes with a soiled Kleenex, "if only I had enough money."

Helmstrand's lecture was winding down. In only two hours, the subject had shifted from Moscow Bolsheviks to Sanscrit and back to the Overstately Powers, a veritable history of civilization illustrating Arian superiority, the fundamental religious and linguistic unity of all Asians and a Jewish conspiracy to control the world. As we stepped ashore in Victoria harbour, his parting shot was a lesson in etymology.

"Your name has nothing to do with a fish; it comes from the Old Norse *gedda*, one who runs amok into battle."

I never saw Helmstrand again, nor any of the others, but I thought about his remarks. This fascist Santa Claus was mad as a hatter, but he was right about one thing. There are no observers, official or unofficial, in this game.

BAKALUK

You could hear the rumble of the bomb
70 miles away.

The Americans dropped
bras and panties—
then food.

First things first.

64

One relief container crashed through a hut
killing a POW.

On the way back home
I saw two movies in the canteen:
Donald Duck and *Frankenstein*.

The ship was called
the USS *Glory*.

14

The cobalt was not working.

The doctor had explained its use when the treatments began. Something about concentrated energy of the sun, con-
tained in molecules or atomic particles, being beamed at the
deadly reproductive cells in her body.

"Think of it as a war. We bombard the enemy cells at a faster
rate than they can reproduce or be replaced by new troops and
we win the war."

He smiles at the aptness of his analogy, pats her arm and
adjusts the cannon of the huge cobalt apparatus so it is aimed
at some point in her lower abdomen. My womb, she thinks,
this is no place for a fight to the finish.

She's read in the morning paper that a delegation of Hong
Kong veterans from BC is going to Ottawa to see the Minister of Veterans Affairs about the long-overdue disability
pensions. One, a former boxer and athlete from Victoria, has
gathered a dossier of documents on medical problems peculiar
to veterans of the Pacific campaign.

Not all the men had come home from the war. Her own had
joined up, after all, and gone to Halifax as a hull inspector.

65

Handsome in his blue uniform, but a little funny and self-important. He survived, but the marriage didn't. A chief petty officer. Just so.

The youngest is in the waiting-room of the clinic, reading comics and eating a bag of licorice. His brother will be on the way home from school to deliver the *Sun*. Ann has agreed to adopt them, it's all settled.

"Do you remember when we were young, Ann, and used to walk our babies together in Stanley Park and talk about our hopes and fears? I said if I died first I'd send you the smell of roses, so you'd know I was nearby."

She recalls the blunt stern of the *Awatea*, as it churned seaward beyond the span of the Lions Gate Bridge, and the number of following gulls. The band was still playing "Good Night, Irene."

15

The atomic blast, which ends one stage
of the ordeal, ushers in another,
rendering life as we know it, and art

impossible. So the poet, dreaming an epic,
produces, Sir, a few meagre voices
and chance fragments, random particles
that don't so much cohere as co-exist,
naked, stripped of familiar defences, but not,
for all that, without meaning or rhyme.

Plucked from the sidelines of history
into the very thick, he battles
insurmountable odds, codes and signifiers

in hand, his characters skirmishing
from particularity toward myth,
attains a little advantage, some elevation

above events, a knoll or redoubt, where,
for a moment, perhaps, he can take stock,
regroup and view his muddied countenance

in a helmetful of rainwater.
Nothing of the shape he dreamed survives,
yet what he is and has imagined

is all there, ragged, dressed in motley,
the patchwork quilt he'd left behind at home,
where every swatch of cloth

contains some precious chunk of memory
not recorded in official documents.
Forgive him, Sir. He has stared too long

at the rising sun, gone blind.
The helmet is a fiction, like so much else,
to free him from the barbs of time.

67